AF473403

FaithSteps

40 Days: A Personal Journey to Renewal of Mind and Spirit

By

Carlond W. Gray

authorHOUSE

1663 Liberty Drive, Suite 200
Bloomington, Indiana 47403
(800) 839-8640
www.authorhouse.com

First published by AuthorHouse 07/06/04

ISBN: 1-4184-2123-5 (e)
ISBN: 1-4184-2124-3 (sc)

Printed in the United States of America
Bloomington, Indiana

This book is printed on acid-free paper.

"Do not be conformed to this world (this age), [fashioned after and adapted to its external, superficial customs], but be transformed (changed) by the [entire] renewal of your mind [by its new ideals and its new attitudes], so that you may prove [for yourselves] what is the good and acceptable and perfect [in His sight for you]"... Romans 12:1,2 (Amplified Bible)

This book is dedicated to the Spirit of Truth that is in all of us.

Thank you for being “The Way, The Truth, and The Light”

Acknowledgements

Honor and Glory to El Elyon, The Most High God. Without that 3:00AM wake-up call on July 7, 2002, this devotional journal would not have been written. He used many people, preachers, teachers, family, friends, and ex-coworkers to birth this devotional journal.

To the Body of Christ who must not "copy the behavior and customs of this world, but let God transform you into a new person by changing the way you think. Then you will know what God wants you to do, and you will know how good and pleasing and perfect his will really is. (Romans 12:1,2)"

To my family, who has played a major role in where I am today, the late Johnnie M. Wright, my mother, who is truly the Spirit of the Virtuous Woman given in Proverbs 31. My precious gift as well as lovely, growing in the spirit, talented daughter, Phenessa A. Gray, who's life continues to exemplify a search for genuine truth, love, joy, peace, and happiness in the Holy Spirit and who showed me it could be done. Thanks for your inspiration and persistence to continue to fight the good fight of faith. To my beautiful gift from God, my granddaughter, Hannah, who gives me motivation to live as an example before her and exemplify a blessing in my life as the son given to Boaz and Ruth that blessed Naomi (Ruth 4). I pray this book will help her to know in the years to come that God has a plan ordained for her. I wait on the day she is able to read this book and give me her revelations.

To My sisters, Julia M. Lamons and Dr. Shirley W. Watson, brothers, Isaac Wright Jr., Rev. James P. Wright, and Jessie Wright and Godfather, Robert Duckworth. May God's riches blessings "come on thee, and overtake thee, as you hearken unto the voice of the Lord thy God. (Deuteronomy 28:2)". All of you are examples of how God moves us from faith to faith!

To my Spiritual sisters, Queen(s) Beverly "BIBI" Clark Acofuss, Annie Seabrooks, and Cheryl Miles, Linda Scott, Brenda Johnson, Estell Benefield, Esther Ashley, Marie Baker, Stella Crawford, Iris Jackson, Cheryl Taylor, Patricia Murdock, Joann Spurlock, Gloria Harrison, and all others who have been in my life from First Baptist Church in Warrington, Florida, Bethel Baptist Institutional Church in Jacksonville, Florida, Shiloh Baptist Church in Baton Rouge, Louisiana, Hopewell Missionary Baptist Church in Norcross, Georgia, and New Birth Missionary Baptist Church in Lithonia, Georgia, thank you for being the light that shineth upon a hill.

To my Spiritual Shepherds, The late Rev. Isaac Wright Sr. and Deacon King Carter, Rev. Rudolph McKissick Sr., Rev. Charles T. Smith, Dr. William L. Sheals, and Bishop Eddie L. Long, without your teaching and leadership, how could I hear without a preacher (Romans 10:14). Thank you for accepting the call of God in your lives. I am grateful for the many years of the unadulterated word of God and your lifelong examples.

There are many that have crossed my path in business, social gatherings, and conferences that I am unable to name. Yet, each one played a major part in my spiritual journey. If you believed, talked about, praised, admired, cursed, prayed for me, you have been apart of this journey. Thank You!

Foreword

We live in a society where chaos and confusion are the norm. Money, power, and sex are this nation's mantra and there is no such thing as "common" sense anymore. Nevertheless, through our trials and tribulations, it is imperative to focus on heavenly things and remember that earthly things are temporal. In order to accomplish this much needed feat, we must renew or mind and spirit daily aggressively meditating on God's Word and practicing to walk in His Way and not our own.

<u>40 Days: A Personal Journey to Renewal of Mind & Spirit</u> is a self-evaluation book that challenges you to look heavenward and not focus on the vicissitudes of life. I am reminded of Job, a godly man who experienced many hardships. Yet, in the midst of it all, he continued to renew his mind and spirit and never doubted our Lord. He stated, "If a man dies, will he live again? All the days of my hard service, I will wait for my renewal to come." (NIV - Job 14:14) Renewing your mind and Spirit is not easy and requires much practice. God never said that it would be easy, just that it would be worth it. My mother's book is not only inspirational but also life-transforming. It aids in this struggle to become rested, rejuvenated, and revived in Christ.

We all have testimonies that shake our souls, but it's comforting to know that we have a God that loved us enough to walk in our shoes and give us hope that through Him life can be lived abundantly despite the toils and snares. My mother is a living witness of that. She speaks from her experiences of weathering the storms of life and conquering the adversities that come against our mind and Spirit. She is a blessing to the Body of Christ and her words of encouragement and restoration in Christ will bless you richly as she shares those lessons she has learned from her life experiences. We are blessed to be a blessing. Thank you, Mom, for blessing me with your words and sharing your gifts with the world. After reading this book, your life will be transformed and the light of Christ will shine as far as the east is from the west.

Miracles & Blessings,

Phenessa A. Gray, Poetess & Author of My Soul's Surrender

Table of Contents

Introduction

Many Christians cry out to God in desperation for understanding. Many believe that this life should be so much more. This desperation for a clearer vision of purpose creates a yearning for renewal and direction for each day. Are you desperately seeking renewal in your life? Are you praying for God's promises to manifest in your life? The answer to both of these questions for me is yes. Out of my desperation, I began to seek God for understanding. Yes, I was already saved but living a mediocre life. I sought God because I believe Bishop Eddie L. Long when he says, "There is a promise to every problem."

How many Christians do you know who are defeated in their finances, marriages, health, jobs, etc.? I admit that I was one of them. I struggled for many years to be free from the bondage of debt so that I could be a blessing to all I meet. Each month, I paid tithes and offerings. Yet, I was defeated financially. It was like verse 6 in Haggai 1, "he that earneth wages earneth wages to put it into a bag with holes." I always asked the question, Why? Perhaps one of the answers is that I lacked the proper financial training during my younger years or I was not disciplined enough to live below my pay. One thing I do know and that is "What you don't know will hurt you."

It is my prayer that this devotional will encourage you in your area of weakness and enable you to commit to working through all of your circumstances and situations as you grasp your vision because "Where there is no vision, the people perish"(Proverbs 29:18). You must grab hold of this truth, "It is the same with my word, I send it out, and it always produces fruit. It will accomplish all I want it to, and it will prosper everywhere I send it (Isaiah 55:11) Amplified Bible. God's word is true, powerful and provides deliverance.

References to forty days are found in Holy Scripture many times. The significance of forty days involves dedication, commitment, and accountability. Forty is the number of building foundations. Jesus' temptation in the wilderness for 40 days is one of the major events in scripture. Satan attempted to destroy Jesus with the lust of the flesh, lust of the eyes, and the pride of life. He continues to use this strategy on you and me today. Moses is another example which is found in Deuteronomy 9:9, "When I was on the mountain receiving the tablets of stone inscribed with the covenant that the Lord had made with you. I was there forty days and forty nights, and all that time I ate nothing and drank no water." But, in verse 12, we see that the Israelites had become corrupt. They cast an idol from gold for themselves. The last example comes from Acts 1:3. This verse tells us that Jesus was seen of the disciples 40 days after He was resurrected speaking of the things pertaining to the Kingdom of God.

If you are looking for a way to spend more time with the Lord, this journal will help you. This 40-Day journey is being shared with all that need encouragement to listen to the Spirit within you and to dedicate time to receive direction for your life. On each page, you are given a "Faith Step" and space to write down your commitments or comments. Also, you can write down blessings you received from taking a "Faith Step." At the end of the 40 days, you will have a record of how and where God brought you. I beseech you, beloved, to use this section diligently.

You will notice several days with references to Psalm 91 and Jeremiah 29:11. These scriptures were the unfolding of God's messages and promises to me. The three main themes are (1) *God's word* is the answer to all your problems and concerns, (2) *God's presence* is more important than anything, and (3) *God's provisions* are manifested through seed, time, and harvest. I pray that you will find each reading a point of inspiration for all your needs!

There Comes A Time

There comes a time
When things must stop
Must change,
Sometimes stay the same
There comes a time
When one must realize
Their purpose in life
Their place in God's Kingdom
When to sit down
Just when to,
The possibility of recognizing wrongs
Continuing to do rights
By others
Most of all, by yourself
Don't let time determine your demise
Before it's too late to give God glory.

Author: ***Phenessa A. Gray*****,** **My Soul's Surrender**

Day 1: 3:00AM Divine Wake-up Call

...he wakeneth morning by morning, he wakeneth mine ear to hear as the learned . - Isaiah 50:4

Sunday morning, July 7, 2002, the Spirit of the Living God awakens me to commit to forty days of renewing my mind and spirit. 3:00AM, I only had two more hours to sleep before getting up to attend early worship service at Hopewell Missionary Baptist Church. Awaken at 3:00AM was the last thing I wanted. Yet, I was wide-awake and couldn't go back to sleep.

The Spirit began to minister to my heart about forty days. Jesus was in the wilderness for 40 days. During that time, He was tempted of the devil to change stones into bread, cast himself down to test God's love for Him, and to worship Satan to receive the world (Matthew 4:1-11). Just as Jesus was tempted, I knew I would be tempted to discontinue or not be true to a forty day commitment to study God's word, meditate on His word, and practice His promises. As I made this commitment, I knew only the power of God within me could sustain me and change me during this forty-day period. I made the commitment to focus my thoughts on things that were "true and honorable, pure and lovely and admirable, excellent and worthy of praise (Philippians 4:8, Amplified)."

As this day proceeded, the battle raged between my mind and my flesh. The battle was like a tennis ball bouncing back and forth across a net. Thank God for His Holy Spirit who convicts and help minds to change.

FaithStep(s): The next time you are awaken in the middle of the night pray and ask God what is it He wants you to do. Make sure you are obedient and do what He instructs you to do. Write this occurrence in your journal.

Personal Note: ____

Personal Note (cont'd): ___________________________

Day 2: How Are You?

I will lift up my eyes unto the hills, from whence cometh my help. My help cometh from the Lord, which made heaven and earth. - Psalm 121:1,2

3:45AM and again, I couldn't sleep. I reached for my daily meditation books. The message for today was taken from Matthew 15: 10-20 and the meditation, "How Are You?" I thought this very appropriate because I had a lot on my mind. Another meditation, "Look Beyond The Hills" gave me direction with the scripture taken from Psalm 121. I knew God was preparing me for the day.

As the day proceeded, I realized how short-tempered and irritable I was. My brother was having problems letting up the shades in the kitchen and then I stepped into cereal and milk that my granddaughter accidently knocked out of my hands. By the end of these occurrences, I realized the battle between flesh and spirit had started. Immediately, the Holy Spirit brought to mind, "This is the day the Lord has made and I will rejoice and be glad in it (Psalm 118:24). In spite of the events that took place, I thought it was time for me to "lift up mine eyes unto the hills from whence cometh my help. My help cometh from the Lord which made heaven and earth (Psalm 121:1-2)."

When difficult situations confront you, remember your help comes from God, The Spirit within you. The Holy Spirit, Comforter and Guide, within you who will lead, guide, and direct your every step if you allow Him.

FaithStep(s): Remember God's word speaks life into every situation in your life. You can reap the blessings of peace that passeth all understanding when you need strength, direction, and comfort.

Personal Note: ______________________________

____

____

____

____

____

____

____

____

____

____

____

____

____

Personal Note (cont'd): ______________________________

Day 3: Reason to Praise

Every day will I bless thee; and I will praise thy name for ever and ever. - Psalm145:2

Praise God for another day's journey! Father, thank you for watching over us as we slept during the night and for your protective angels. "It was you who laid the foundations of the earth, determined the dimensions, provided support, laid the cornerstone as the morning stars sang together, and defined the boundaries of the sea (Job 38:1-10)." What a Mighty God we serve! He is surely Creator, Redeemer, Sustainer, Lord, Saviour, and Provider.

In order to recognize and acknowledge the true character of God, we must surrender our will for His will. Allow the Fruit of the Spirit- love, joy, peace, longsuffering, kindness, goodness, meekness and temperance (Galatians 5:22,23) - to grow in your life more than any thing else in the world. When love has become perfect or mature, you will begin to see the Fruit of the Spirit in your daily lives. You will be confronted with many situations to take you off course but you must make up in your mind never to give up. You must decide to keep moving forward. What's your reason(s) to praise?

FaithStep(s): Write down your praise report. You may want to journal each day for one (1) week and the blessings God gives to you.

Personal Note: ______________________________

Day 4: Taking Time with God

Wherefore take unto you the whole armour of God, that ye may be able to withstand in the evil day, and having done all, to stand. - Ephesians 6:13

God confirms His direction in many ways. As I listened to teaching on the topic, Spiritual Warfare of Rest, and Renewing Your Mind, it became clear to me what the next 36 days would bring about in my life. Renewing of the mind always bring about spiritual warfare. Spending time with God will always give victory in both of these areas.

Psalm 119:105, "Your word is a lamp for my feet and a light for my path." provides the tool to use when taking time with God. The more you are in the word of God, the more you will become aware that your steps are order by Him (Psalm 37:23). Not only are your steps ordered but also God takes delight in you. You can experience His presence and walk in His righteousness. There is no joy like being in the presence of God. Knowing that you can cast your cares upon Him because He cares for you (1 Peter 5:7). Hallelujah!

How much time do you spend with God? How much time do you spend at work, with friends, family, etc.? Is your time in the world more than the time you spend with God?

FaithStep(s): Work toward spending 10% of your time each day with the Lord then increase it over time.

Personal Note: ______________________________

Personal Note (cont'd): ______________________________

Day 5: Confirmation

And they went forth, and preached every where, the Lord working with them, and confirming the word with signs following. - Mark 16:20

Confirmation, Confirmation, Confirmation. God's message for this day is about the protection of God. An inspirational writing, Our Dwelling Place, found in the Women Devotional Bible written by Hope MacDonald encourages readers to read Psalm 91 for 30 days. After reading it, I heard Joyce Meyer instruct the audience to turn to Psalm 91. Once again, the Holy Spirit continued to speak through each devotional I read. Each of these readings confirmed to me that reading and meditating on Psalm 91 for the next 30 days is God's direction for me.

The New King James Version of "The Open Bible" says, "Psalm 91 appears to be a composite of a wisdom poem (vv. 1-13) and a divine oracle (vv. 14-16). It speaks of the security that the Messiah and His followers may find in God." We need to know that God is an abiding place for us in this rebellious world. The secret place of God is the only protection and safe haven for us.

What is God confirming in your life today? Are you taking the time to hear from Him? Are you using head knowledge instead of being directed by the Spirit of God: If your steps are not being confirmed, slow down and wait for God's direction. If you need help hearing or understanding God's direction, seek spiritual help.

FaithStep(s): Take 5-10 minutes to review your day. Is God confirming a message to you?

Personal Note: ____

____

____

____

____

____

____

____

____

____

____

____

____

____

____

____

____

____

Personal Note (cont'd):

Day 6: Psalm 91

These things I have spoken unto you, that in me ye might have peace. In the world ye shall have tribulation: but be of good cheer; I have overcome the world. - John 16:33

The Bible is filled with the promises of God. Psalm 91 covers every aspect of living. The only requirement is to "dwell in the secret place of the Most High (vv.1)". The secret place for me today is in prayer. Matthew 6:6 declares that "when you pray, go away by yourself, shut the door behind you, and pray to your Father secretly. Then your Father, who knows all secrets, will reward you."

The promises of Psalm 91 provide encouragement to those who feel trapped and need a Deliverer. Jesus is that Deliverer from the fears of this world's ills. He's the hope for the hopeless, faith for the fearful, and strength for the weak. No matter what the need of His children, He is able to provide.

What are you in need of today? No matter what it is, your Father in Heaven is able to do exceedingly, abundantly above all we ask or think, according to the power that worketh in us (Ephesians 3:20)." Call on that power today!

FaithStep(s): Commit to reading, meditating, and confessing Psalm 91 from day-to- day and see God's power work in your life.

Personal Note: ______________________________

Personal Note (cont'd): ______________________________

Day 7: Worship Is My Opportunity

O come, let us worship and bow down: let us kneel before the Lord our maker. - Psalm 95:6

What really matters? As I read this daily meditation from the Daily Bread, I believe with inferential men like Benjamin Franklin, Abraham Lincoln, Theodore Roosevelt, and Martin Luther King that worship of the Most High God matters. Of course, each one must answer this question for themselves.

Worship of the one true living God manifests love, joy, peace, longsuffering, kindness, goodness, meekness, faithfulness, and self-control (Galatians 5:22,23) in our lives. To grow in the Fruit of the Spirit, it's essential to fellowship with other believers. The local Body of Christ is the one place where the focus is on worshipping God the Father, God the Son, and God the Holy Spirit. The result of this focus brings the Fruit of the Spirit that kindles in our hearts and the hearts of all we meet. Let us not forget the importance of worshipping and meeting God each day.

FaithStep(s): Read all of the scriptures about worship and then practice worshipping God each day.

Personal Note:

Personal Note (cont'd):

Day 8: Faith Is the Key

Now faith is the substance of things hoped for, the evidence of things not seen. - Hebrews 11:1

The number 8 is the spiritual symbol for a new beginning. On this eighth day of my forty-day journey to spiritual and mental renewal, the answer to true success is my faith in the living Lord. A faith that has brought me from September 28, 2001, the day I retired, to this day. A faith in Jehovah Jireh, Provider, who has proven to be faithful and Provider of health, wealth, and prosperity. A faith that God is working all things together for my good (Romans 8:28).

This faith has helped me to rely on "The Master's Hand" that is in all the events and the provisions of each day. His hand has protected (Psalm 91), provided peace that surpasseth all understanding (Philippians 4:7), and has made provisions for each day (Philippians 4:19). I go forward unafraid.

What are you in need of today? Can you step out on your faith and receive it, today?

FaithStep(s): Determine the measure of your faith and put it into action for the promises and blessings of a living Saviour, today.

Personal Note: ______________________________________

Personal Note (cont'd): ________________________________

Day 9: Life and Death

He that speaketh truth sheweth forth righteousness: but a false witness deceit. - Proverbs 12:17

The New Living Translation of Proverbs 18:21 says, "those who love to talk will experience the consequences, for the tongue can kill or nourish life, makes it clear how much power you have over your life." Are you aware of how much power you have over your life? If worry, lack, sickness, or confusion is apart of your day, then maybe you should take a few minutes to check out what you are thinking and saying.

Again, confirmation from two messages, "Dressed for Battle" and "Seven Keys to Success", support the need to speak life to my life. How is that done? *The Word of God is the only way.* Whatever the concern or situation, the living Word of God has the answer. If you don't have a study bible, concordance or bible dictionary, buy one today. The next step is to take time to read, meditate, and practice the Word of God in your life everyday.

Remember, life and death are in the power of the tongue (Proverbs 18:21).

FaithStep(s): Speak life into your life by using the Word of God minute by minute, second by second of each day.

What steps will you take *today* to change your circumstances?

Personal Note: ____

Personal Note (cont'd):

Day 10: Psalm 18: 1-6

In my distress I called upon the Lord, and cried unto my God: he heard my voice out of his temple, and my cry came before him, even into his ears. - Psalm 18:5

David cried out to the Lord for help in Psalm 18:1-6 to express his love, appreciation, and trust in the Lord. It is true; God's help is only a prayer away. This Psalm ushered me into a prayer for a closer intimacy with Him. Yes, I need His provisions, protection, and presence but I need to know Him better. When we know Him, nothing else matters. In knowing Him, we began to understand His covenant with us. The Abrahamic Covenant provides all of our needs, wants, and desires.

The Abrahamic Covenant is found in Genesis 12. This covenant is for the saints of God today. The study of this covenant will help you to know who you are in Christ Jesus. It will give you love, appreciation, and trust in the Lord. Do you know your covenant rights? Are you aware of whom you are in Christ Jesus? If not, God's word will help you to know who you are and to walk in your calling.

FaithStep(s): Read Genesis 12 and receive your covenant with God. Express your love, appreciation, and trust in the God of Abraham, Isaac, and Jacob.

Personal Note: ______________________________

Personal Note (cont'd):

Day 11: Receive God's Love

That if thou shalt confess with thy mouth the Lord Je'sus, and shalt believe in thine heart that God hath raised him from the dead, thou shalt be saved. - Romans 10:9

"Love is a decision to do the will of God and a spiritual tool to defeat satan (Joyce Meyer)." As Joyce taught how to receive God's love, my spirit was touched. Many times we take God's love for granted. Do you really realize what God has done for you? John 3:16 tells us, "For God so loved the world that He gave His only begotten Son, that whosoever believeth in Him should not perish, but have everlasting life." If He gave His only son, there is nothing else He will not do for you.

If you have not received God's precious gift of love, now is the time. All you have to do is say this prayer:

> Jesus, I believe that you are the holy Son of God. I believe that you died on the cross for my sins and that you rose from the dead. You are my salvation. Please come into my life and wash all my sins away and make me a child of God. I give my life to you completely today. In Jesus name, Amen

If you prayed this prayer and really meant it in your heart, you are saved. You are in the household of faith (Galatians 6:10). Welcome to the Body of Christ! Remember, "God so loved the world that He gave His only begotten Son, that whosoever believeth in him should not perish, but have everlasting life (John 3:16)". You are whosoever!

FaithStep(s): Write the date and time down you prayed this prayer then read the Gospels of Matthew, Mark, Luke, John and Romans to get to know and experience the life of Jesus and what salvation really is for those who accept Him. Find a local Fellowship/ church to attend to learn about Christ and what he has for *you* to do!

Personal Note: ________________________________

____

____

____

____

____

____

____

____

____

____

____

Personal Note (cont'd):

Day 12: The Whole Armour of God

Put on the whole armour of God, that ye may be able to stand against the wiles of the devil. - Ephesians 6:11

In the Christian walk, we must have an offense and defense. Ephesians 6:1-18 gives us all that we need to walk in victory. The belt of *truth* will keep you free from sin. *Righteousness* will keep you in the will of God. *Peace* only comes from the Word of God to keep you prepared to live each day. *Faith* is the shield to stop the fiery arrows aimed at you by Satan. *Salvation* to guard your mind and the S*word of the Spirit,* the Word of God, to renew your mind daily. Prayer will keep you alert and build up the Body of Christ everywhere (NLT).

To seal this message of God for me today, Strength and Service, provided this prayer written by Floyd Allan Bash:

> Heavenly Father, Thou art my refuge and strength. I know I am not able to beat down temptation if I have to do it alone. I want the irresistible Spirit that raised Jesus from the dead to dwell in my heart. Come in, Spirit of God, to my heart, and take control. Grant me spiritual power, for Jesus' sake. Amen.

FaithStep(s): Practice putting on the whole armor of God, Truth, Righteousness, Peace, Faith, Salvation, and the Sword of the Spirit. Confess this armor each day. Confess daily, I will walk in truth, righteousness, peace, faith, and salvation with the Word of God.

Personal Note: ______________________________________

____

____

____

____

____

____

____

____

____

____

____

____

____

____

____

____

____

____

Personal Note (cont'd):

Day 13: Building A New House

But he answered and said, It is written, Man shall not live by bread alone, but by every word that proceedeth out of the mouth of God. - Matthew 4:4

Except the Lord build the house, they labour in vain that build it (Psalm 127:1). As I awaken this morning by the hammering of the workmen next door who are building a new house, I was reminded that unless Christians build their daily life on the truth of God's word, they will return to the things that are taught by the world. From preschool through college, students are taught how to make a living not how to live. Christians must begin to teach their children how to live according to God's word. The word of God will provide a living because He is Jehovah Jireh (Genesis 22: 13-14). All through the Bible, God provided for His people. Not only the Israelites but Gentiles as well who believed His word and practiced it in their daily lives.

Hope McDonald writes in Our Dwelling Place that God's "unchanging promises are for those who choose, by an act of their will to put themselves under the care and protection of the living God. These promises are for those who dwell within the shelter of the Most High, who make their home with Jesus." If you're building a new life in Christ or have been a Christian for many years, your living manual is the living Word of God.

FaithStep(s): Read Deuteronomy 8: 1-3 and meditate on verse 3.

Personal Note: ______________________________________

Personal Note (cont'd):

Day 14: All the Wrong Notes

Trust in the Lord with all thine heart; and lean not unto thine own understanding. In all thy ways acknowledge him, and he shall direct thy path. - Proverbs 3:5,6

Written notes or musical notes can be heard or written wrong. The wrong written notes will give you the wrong understanding. The wrong musical note will make the song unbearable. How many times do we see Christians taking notes during a sermon, conference, or class? Are you one of them? If so, make sure your notes are correct. Make sure your notes give you clear directions.

I attended a conference on this fourteenth day which provided several good steps to success and I would like to share them with you below.

1. Be Consistent
2. Be Coachable
3. Be Connected
4. Be Committed

I believe these steps can be applied to your walk with the Lord. Be consistent in the study, reading, and practice of God's word. Be coachable by those who teach, preach, and are good examples of God's Word. Be connected to the Holy Spirit. Be Committed to bearing good fruit (Galatians 5:22-23) in your life.

FaithStep(s): Inventory your daily schedule and determine if you are living according to God's will for your life. If not, start today making changes.

Personal Note: ______________________________

Personal Note (cont'd):

Day 15: The Way of Praise

Let every thing that hath breath praise the Lord. Praise ye the Lord. - Psalm 150:6

Many times we wonder what it's going to take for us to walk in the victory of God. We often feel defeated rather than victorious. *When* you are feeling defeated, depressed, unworthy, "The way to remove mountains is the way of Praise. *When* trouble comes think of all you have to be thankful. Praise, Praise, Praise (God's Calling)."

If you read the Psalms written by David, you will readily see that when David petitioned God, talked about his enemies, he ended each Psalm with praise to God. Remember, Praising God will release your burden and direct your care toward the one who can and will not withhold any good thing from them that walk uprightly (Psalm 84:11). When you accepted Jesus Christ as your Lord and Saviour, you became the righteousness of God and must give Him praise because He is worthy to be praised!

FaithStep(s): Whatever your need is today, go to God in prayer and give the best praise you know how to give.

Personal Note:

Personal Note (cont'd):

Day 16: Be True To Thyself

If it be so, our God whom we serve is able to deliver us from the burning fiery furnace, and he will deliver us out of thine hand, O king. - Daniel 3:17

Daniel is a good example of being true to yourself. Faced with many opportunities to conform to the environment where he was placed; he decided to stay true to himself and the God he served. How did he do this? He obeyed the commandments of God. Daniel 1:8 says "But Daniel purposed in his heart that he would not defile himself." We must, also, purpose in our hearts to walk holy and acceptable to God.

Are you faced with situations that jeopardize your commitment and holiness before God? Are you facing challenges in life that may defile you? Do you have the Holy Spirit to guide you? Whatever the circumstance, you must purpose in your heart to please God. He will give you the victory!

FaithStep(s): Take time to pray about any circumstances, situations, or challenges in your life that compromise your walk with the Lord. Start this moment to eliminate them in your life by lining up with the Word of God.

Personal Note:

Personal Note (cont'd):____

Day 17: Take Heed

Keep thy heart with all diligence; for out of it are the issues of life. - Proverbs 4:23

Paul admonishes Timothy in 1 Timothy 4:16 to "take heed unto thyself, and unto the doctrine; continue in them: for in doing this thou shalt both save thyself and them that hear thee." Take heed simply means to keep a close watch. Why? Because "For as he thinketh in his heart, so is he: (Proverbs 23:7)."

P. H. Welshimer writes three statements for our consideration about taking heed in Strength and Service. One, to take heed unto your speech. The Bible says "Life and Death are in the power of the tongue (Proverbs 18:21). Speech can betray you and "impressions are made by one's words and deeds. Two, take heed unto thy conduct. Christians must walk holy before God and remember that man looks on the outer appearance, but God looks on the heart (1 Samuel 16:7). Three, take heed to your prayer life. "More things are wrought by prayer than this world dream of." "Prayer changes things." "Pray without ceasing." "The effectual fervent prayer of a righteous man availeth much (James 5:16)."

If you are mindful of your speech, your conduct, and your prayer life, you will experience the victory of holiness before God and in Christ Jesus every second of the day.

FaithStep(s): One day out of the month, make a conscious effort to be mindful of your thoughts, words and actions. If there is anything that hinders your spiritual growth, take steps to eliminate it from your life.

Personal Note: ______________________________

Personal Note (cont'd):

Day 18: Jeremiah 29:11-14

And I will give thee the treasures of darkness, and hidden riches of secret places, that thou mayest know that I, the Lord, which call thee by thy name, am the God of Israel. - Isaiah 45, 3

Are you aware of God's plans for you? Jeremiah 29:11-14 in the New International Version tells us:

> "For I know the plans I have for you, declares the Lord, plans to prosper you and not to harm you, plans to give you hope and a future. Then you will call upon me and come and pray to me, and I will listen to you. You will seek me and find me when you seek me with all your heart. I will be found by you, declares the Lord, and will bring you back from captivity."

His plans are clearly written in this word. None of us should question again, What are God's plan for my life. What we should ask as we seek the Lord with all our hearts is, Where is the place you have prepared for me? Help me to see in the spiritual what you have prepared for me to be manifested in the physical.

Thank you, Father God, for the plans you have for our lives. Plans to prosper us and not to harm. When life is difficult, help us to remember that you have plans that no man, situation, or circumstance can alter.

FaithStep(s): Confess Jeremiah 29:11-14 daily and journal God's goodness to you.

Personal Note: ____________________________________

Personal Note (cont'd):

Day 19: Wonderful Life

Be careful for nothing; but in every thing by prayer and supplication with thanksgiving let your request be made known unto God. - Philippians 4:6

Jeremiah 29:11-14 and Psalm 91 are major scriptures to obtaining and living a wonderful life. The Lord in these scriptures is the Provider, Protector, and Controller of our days, for the Present and the Future. A life that is God-taught and God-guided is one that will allow us to shed light not a shadow everywhere we go.

There will be times when adversities will come. Our only weapon is the Word of God. We can ask God anything! We should pray from our heart and speak the truth of God's word. God honors His word as we make it our first response. Instead of worrying or fretting, pray to God with a sincere heart.

We serve an awesome God who provides a wonderful life and no evil can destroy you. Today receive His power, presence, and provisions for a wonderful life.

FaithStep(s): Read Jeremiah 29:11-14 and Psalm 91. Pray without ceasing the promises for the wonderful life He has provided.

Personal Note: ______________________________

Personal Note (cont'd): ________________________________

Day 20: Your Place in Time

Then the devil leaveth him, and, behold, angels came and ministered unto him. - Matthew 4:11

Have you ever had a dream that made a dramatic impression on you? A dream that changed your day? I was awaken from a dream about 7:30AM. The dream involved a prophet of God laying His hands on me. It felt like a drill penetrating my skull. I believe this dream was a confirmation from God that He is renewing my mind.

It is not to my surprise that as the day progressed, discouragement tried to overtake me. Because God's word is settled in my spirit and is renewing my mind, I spoke its truth throughout the day. Every time an unholy thought attacked, I spoke the Holy Word. The best example of speaking God's word is in the scriptures about Jesus in the Wilderness (Matthew 4: 1-11). After each proposition of Satan, Jesus said, "It is written." You and I must also use the power of the written word.

Whatever your challenges, circumstances, or situations are today, find the Word of God that declares your victory. It is written for you. You have the victory because Jesus paid the price. Remember, Jesus said, "You shall have tribulations in the world but be of good cheer, I have overcome the world (John 16:33)".

FaithStep(s): Confess God's truth in your challenges, circumstances, or situations and it will come to past.

Personal Note: ________________________________

Personal Note (cont'd): ________________________________

Day 21: Holy Is The Lord!

Therefore being justified by faith, we have peace with God through our Lord Jesus Christ: whom also we have access by faith into this grace wherein we stand, and rejoice in hope of the glory of God. - Romans 5:1,2

Holy is the Lord and greatly to be praised! Why praise? Because of who He is. He is the only true God, three in one and who is all powerful, all knowing, and always present. When you call, He will answer (Isaiah 65:24). When you need Him, He is there for you.

His names are listed below for you to become familiar with His character. We must know God in order to serve Him.

El Shaddai - All-Sufficient One (Genesis 17:1-20)

El Elyon - The Most High God (Isaiah 14:13-14)

El Olam - The Everlasting God (Isaiah 40:28)

El Roi - The One Who Seeth (Genesis 16:13)

Elohim - Creator (Ecclesiates 12:1)

Adonai - Lord, Master (Isaiah 1:24)

Yahweh - Lord Jehovah (Exodus 6:3)

Qanna - Jealous (Exodus 34:14)

Jehovah - Self-Existent One (Exodus 3:14)

Jehovah-Nissi - The Lord My Banner (Exodus 17:15,16)

Jehovah-Raah - The Lord My Shepherd (Psalm 23:1)

Jehovah-Rapha - The Lord that Healeth (Genesis 20:17, Psalm 107:20)

Jehovah-Shalom - The Lord is Peace (Judges 6:23,24)

Jehovah-Sabaoth - The Lord of Hosts (1 Samuel 1:3)

Jehovah-Tsidkenu - The Lord our Righteousness (Jeremiah 23:6)

Jehovah-Mekoddishkem - The Lord who Sanctifies You (Exodus 31:13)

Jehovah Jireh - The Lord will Provide (Genesis 22:13-14)

There is no situation or circumstance that God can not handle. If you need Him today, call on Him. He's waiting to meet your every need. Remember, He's a Holy God and greatly to be praised! He gave His only begotten Son so that you could be in right relationship with Him. There is nothing He won't do for you if you ask and believe you've received it.

FaithStep(s): Meditate on the name of God that meets your need. Read the scripture that's associated with your need and His name.

Personal Note:

Day 22: Keep on Pressing

I press toward the mark for the prize of the high calling of God in Christ Jesus. - Philippians 3:14

The Sermon delivered today reminded me of the statement I embraced when I retired. The scripture printed on the announcements and invitations was taken from Philippians 3 12-14. This scripture represented the transition I was making. It was time to forget all the situations that were not pleasant as well as the good times. Life was taking another path. I had to press toward the future and to follow God's direction.

Are you in a transition? Are you embracing the change or toiling with it? If it's that time in your life for change, don't fear. Jesus will not leave you or forsake you. If He's directing you into a different space, He will provide the door for you.

Keep on pressing! The best is yet to come. Your faith will keep you moving in the right direction. When you are persuaded that you are being directed by the Holy Spirit, take the next step and be obedient. Obedience is better than sacrifice (1 Samuel 15:22).

FaithStep(s): Take the next step and walk by faith. You are not alone.

Personal Note:

Personal Note (cont'd): ___

Day 23: The Joy of the Lord

...for the joy of the Lord is your strength. - Nehemiah 8:10

The joy of the Lord is something all of us want to have every minute of the day. Some say it's not possible to walk in the presence of the Lord every minute of the day. But, God's word says, "Therefore, since we have been justified through faith, we have peace with God through our Lord Jesus Christ, through whom we have gained access by faith into this grace in which we now stand (Romans 5:1,2)." God provides us with twenty-four, seven access to Him. It's up to us to maintain that access.

How do we maintain access with God? We do it through applying the Word of God to every situation in our lives, praying without ceasing (1 Thessalonians 5:17), and believing God and His Word (Romans 5:1, 15:13) as He changes our relationship and provides inner peace. We begin to live by the power of His Spirit and work toward producing the Fruit of the Spirit, love, joy, peace, longsuffering, kindness, goodness, faithfulness, gentleness, and self-control (Galatians 5: 16, 22-23) in our lives each day. With God's help, we can always do what is right (Romans 14:17).

This revelation about access to God helps us to endure the suffering of this present age. Yet, suffering is not the only path into God's kingdom but there are times when joy will bring us into the Kingdom. Through suffering or joy, access to God is only provided through the acceptance of His Son, Jesus Christ. Are you maintaining your access to a loving, compassionate, holy, and righteous God? He is always present!

FaithStep(s): Make a conscious effort to have joy through the access given you through Jesus Christ.

Personal Note: ______________________________

____

____

____

____

____

____

____

____

____

____

____

____

____

____

Personal Note (cont'd): ______________________________

Day 24: The Final Good

God is faithful, by whom ye were called unto the fellowship of his Son Jesus Christ our Lord. - 1 Corinthians 1:9

All of the patriarches of the Old Testament would attest to Romans 8:28 if we could call them forth today. Daniel in the Lion's Den, Shadrach, Meshach, and Abednego in the fiery furnace, or the children of Israel at Sinai before reaching the promise land. Today, you may be hurting from lost of a love one, a miscarriage, a broken relationship or financial problems. Remember, God is faithful and "We know that all things work together for good to them that love God, to them who are the called according to His purpose." He may not come when we want Him but He's always on time. Purpose in your heart to be like Job in chapter 14, verse 14, "All of the days of my appointed time will I wait, till my change come." Beloved, be encouraged, God has not forgotten you.

Prayer: Father, Creator of heaven and earth, in the name of Jesus, bless the one reading this meditation with assurance of your presence, power, provisions and peace. In the name of Jesus, help them to know that "No weapon formed against them will prosper" and "weeping endures for a night but Joy comes in the morning." Speak life into every circumstance or situation grieving their hearts and minds. By the power of your Holy Spirit lead them into your presence where there is fullness of joy. Thank you, Father, for your faithfulness. In Jesus Name, Amen.

FaithStep(s): Memorize and meditate on Romans 8:28 for one week and give praise to God for all the circumstances or situations in your life.

Personal Note: ____________________________

Personal Note (cont'd):

Day 25: Being Content in a World Like This

Not that I speak in respect of want: for I have learned, in whatsoever state I am, therewith to be content. - Philippians 4:11

What does it take to be content in a world like we have today? A world with threats of terrorism, massive job lost and corrupt corporate scandals. I believe the insights written below by Kimbrough can provide ways to be content.

> "To be content to live in a world like this, one must build himself a world within a world, an inner temple of peace and harmony, a sanctuary where communion can be had with the Most High God, and an understanding of the meaning of our relationship can be reached in the light of God's far-off design for a world out of joint."

The Lord is our refuge and strength (Psalm 27:1) and in times of disarray, we must seek Him. Being grateful for the life we possess when life seems hard helps us to step out of darkness into His marvelous light. Gratitude will lift up our heart and spirit to see the awesome God we serve. He is our Shepherd and watches over us every second of the day (Psalm 23). Seeking inner peace and harmony, communing with the Most High God, and being grateful are the ways to reach contentment when living in a world of confusion.

FaithStep(s): Spend 15 minutes each day giving thanks to God for all He is and for all He is doing in your life.

Personal Note: ______________________________________

Personal Note (cont'd): ______________________________

Day 26: Hebrews 11:6

But without faith it is impossible to please him: for he that cometh to God must believe that he is, and that he is a rewarder of them that diligently seek him. - Hebrews 11:6

Recently, I heard a Bishop say that "faith is a conviction or persuasion with corresponding action." Hebrews 11:6 tells us that we must believe that God exist and He is a rewarder of them that diligently seek Him. Are you convinced or persuaded that God exist? Are you taking corresponding action by diligently seeking Him? No matter what you are seeking Him for, "He is able to do exceedingly, abundantly above what you asked or think according to the power that works in you (Ephesians 3:20)."

This faith is available to you and I when we accept Jesus Christ as Lord and Saviour. This is the first step that enables us to walk in faith. If you just look around, the heavens and earth are visible proof of a God who has all power. There is only one God who has the power to speak light into a dark situation. You can have that power now, today, as you step out on your faith and become intimate with the holy, righteous, loving, and compassionate God of the Bible.

FaithStep(s): Write down what faith is to you. Find scriptures that support your conviction or persuasion.

PersonalNote:

Personal Note (cont'd):

Day 27: Another Chance at Life

I call heaven and earth to record this day against you, that I have set before you life and death, blessing and cursing: therefore choose life, that both thou and your seed may live.Deuteronomy 30:19

Good Morning! Good Evening! Another day to walk in your destiny. Do you know what God has for you to do? Have you inquired of Him?

Many people are confused about life. What is life? Webster says, "life is an organismic state characterized by capacity of metabolism, growth, reaction to stimuli, and reproduction." This definition includes all of your physical, mental, emotional, and intellectual being. Spiritually, life is a state that transcends physical death. From these definitions, we see that there are two aspects of life, physical and spiritual. Physical life comes from the process of reproduction. Spiritual life comes from an encounter with God the Father, God the Son, and God the Holy Spirit. This encounter brings you face-to-face with the question of eternal life or eternal damnation. Eternal life (John 3:16, Romans 10:9) comes with the acceptance of Jesus Christ as the Son of God or eternal damnation (Luke 16:19-21) that is separation from God forever. Forever is a long time! God gives all of us freewill. The choice is yours! Life or death?

FaithStep(s): Chose this very moment where you want to eternally spend the rest of your life. If you have questions, call someone who may be able to answer them.

Personal Note: ___________________________________

____

____

____

____

____

____

____

____

____

____

____

____

____

____

____

____

____

____

Personal Note (cont'd): ______________________________

Day 28: 3:30AM Divine Wake-Up Call

Then shall the King say unto them on his right hand, Come, ye blessed of my Father, inherit the kingdom prepared for you from the foundation of the world: - Matthew 25:34

God's early morning calls are times of prayer and listening for direction. As I sat on the sofa in my living room, I prayed for God's will to be done. His will as I approach each day by faith. Faith that "God will provide all my needs according to His riches in glory by Christ Jesus (Philippians 4:19)." Faith that I have been redeemed by the blood of Jesus and I shall walk in health, wealth, and prosperity. Faith that He will give me double for my trouble. Faith that He who began a good work in me will continue unto the day of Jesus Christ (Philippians 1:6).

The years have been long and tedious but through it all, God provided and delivered. He has made a great investment in me and He will not forfeit His investment or leave me now. Seventeen years ago, He lead me to Matthew 25:34 and from that night on, I have taken His guidance seriously. The entire 25th chapter of Matthew provides direction for my life. Verses 35 and 36 specifically tells me to feed the hungry, give water to the thirsty, invite strangers into my life, clothes the naked, visit the sick and those in prisons. I may not do all of these with my physical presence but I can support ministries that provide these services.

What is God directing you to do today? If you're not sure, pray alone with someone you trust until you are sure of His guidance. "Obedience is better than sacrifice (1 Samuel 15:22)."

FaithStep(s): Praise God for Who He is and for all He is to you. Each day seek His guidance for your life.

Personal Note: ____

____

____

____

____

____

____

____

____

____

____

____

____

____

____

Personal Note (cont'd): ______________________________

Day 29: Is There One?

For I was an hungred, and ye gave me meat: I was thirsty, and ye gave me drink: I was a stranger, and ye took me in: Naked, and ye clothed me:… - Matthew 25:35,36

"Run up and down every street in Jerusalem," says the Lord, "Look high and low; search throughout the city! If you can find even one person who is just and honest, I will not destroy the city (Jeremiah 5:1)." This passage could create uneasiness in Christians today. The world seems to be corrupt on every side. Is there one righteous person?

Yes, there is one. There are people who love justice and seek the truth. There are those who "Bear one another's burdens (Galatians 6:2)." September 11th proved to Americans that there are those who express love and concern for others. During the Christmas season of each year, people who are usually rude and grouchy all during the year, treat others with respect and concern. During hurricanes, tornadoes, fires, or stormy weather, there are those who extend support to others. There is one! Yet, we have room to improve. A majority is not needed, just one. Are you the one?

FaithStep(s): Contribute your time, talent, and/or treasure to help someone today.

Personal note: ______________________________________

____

____

____

____

____

____

____

____

____

____

____

____

____

____

____

____

____

____

____

____

____

Personal Note (cont'd): ______________________________

Day 30: Focus

For as he thinketh in his heart, so is he: Eat and drink, saith he to thee; but his heart is not with thee. - Proverbs 23:7

What you focus on determines what you see or the action you may take. Paul says to the Philippians, "Finally, brethren, whatsoever things are true, whatsoever things are honest, whatsoever things are just, whatsoever things are pure, whatsoever things are lovely, whatsoever things are of good report; if there be any virtue, and if there be any praise, think on these things (Philippians 4:8)." These are good instructions from Paul for Christians to follow each day. When a problem arises in your life, think about the steps Jesus would take to eliminate the problem rather than focusing on the problem. Instead of worrying about what you don't have, focus on what you do have and the blessings of God. Purposely remember the tough times God brought you through in the past. Surely, he will deliver you now.

It is easy to focus on the negatives rather than the positives. Keep your mind on the things that strengthen truth, confidence, hope, nobility, righteousness, holiness, purity, and love. Practice applying these virtues daily. Always focus on belief and refuse to allow your mind to entertain unbelief (Mark 9:24). Ask God to create in you a clean heart and renew a right spirit (Psalm 51:

10) and He will. If you focus on whatsoever is true, honest, pure, lovely, and of a good report, you won't have time for anything else.

FaithStep(s): Practice applying Philippians 4:8 to your concerns today. Journal your concerns and the date when God answers.

Personal Note: ______________________________

____

____

____

____

____

____

____

____

____

____

____

____

____

____

____

Personal Note (cont'd):

Day 31: Suffering

These things I have spoken unto you, that in me ye might have peace. In the world ye shall have tribulation: but be of good cheer; I have overcome the world. - John 16:33

There was a time in my life that I refused to believe that Christians had to suffer. Suffering is one of those experiences in life that is difficult to embrace. Yet, Jesus warned the disciples about the suffering He would endure (Luke 9:18-23). In verse 23 of Luke 9, He sets the requirement for those who would follow Him. "If any man will come after me, let him deny himself, and take up his cross daily, and follow me. Denying oneself and taking up your cross come in many daily experiences. Suffering can be found when you are ignored by associates because you won't laugh at dirty jokes, you maybe overlooked for a promotion because you don't meet coworkers after work for a drink, or you won't celebrate holidays in the fashion that is done by the world. In these times, praying without ceasing and reading God's Word will bring you the strength and the inner peace you need. Don't get discouraged! It's just a test.

After 17 years, I have come to embrace suffering. I see as I look back that in those times when persecutions happened, I ran to the Rock for strength and direction. These times were difficult and even today, suffering is difficult. But, I appreciate the hard times and draw closer to my Saviour.

You, too, will grow stronger during the times of suffering. When God is taking us through the fire, it is for a greater good. Take up your cross daily and follow Jesus as you grow spiritually.

FaithStep(s): When sufferings occur, pray, read your Bible, and praise God.

Personal Note: ______________________________

____

____

____

____

____

____

____

____

____

____

____

____

____

____

Personal Note (cont'd):

Day 32: All Is Well!

Say ye to the righteous, that it shall be well with him: for they shall eat the fruit of their doings. - Isaiah 3:10

Deuteronomy 28 lists promises of blessings and curses. These blessings or curses are executed by our inner life. Within each of us lies the choice of obedience or disobedience. The way of obedience provides the promises of blessings and the way of disobedience provides the promises of curses. It's your choice!

The choice of obedience gives life more abundantly (John 10:10). This life is not only physical and material but spiritually. A spiritually abundant life will help you to be victorious over every circumstance in your life. It moves you from glory to glory (2 Corinthians 3:18) as you are being transformed by the Spirit of the Lord and the renewing of your mind.

The choice of disobedience brings forth eternal separation from God. Life separated from God forever. Your spirit is cast out, withered, and burned (John 15:6). A life filled with darkness and confusion.

I encourage you to accept an abundant life that will give you power to say each day "All is Well!"

FaithStep(s): Instead of saying "fine" when asked, "How are you", say "All is Well" . Say it until it becomes as natural as breathing.

Personal Note: ______________________________

Personal Note (cont'd):

Day 33: Total Surrender

...O my Father, if it be possible, let this cup pass from me: nevertheless not as I will, but as thou wilt. - Matthew 26:39

At the age of 33, Jesus totally surrendered to the Will of God. He fulfilled His ordained mission here on earth. Today, you may be faced with the decision of total surrender. Are you willing to totally surrender to the will of God?

Total surrender means to rely on Jesus alone and ask no help from others. This surrendering to the guidance of the Holy Spirit involves "trusting in the Lord with all your heart, and leaning not on your own understanding; in all your ways acknowledge Him, and He shall direct your paths (Proverb 3:5,6)". This is not saying He will not use others to help you but you must make Him your first response. God is faithful and will not hold back any good thing from His children (Psalm 84:11). That's one reason you don't have to hold back from Him,

God gives us the Law of Divine Supply but you can not receive it until you surrender to Him all of you. The Law of Divine Supply requires you to empty yourself, to totally surrender all to God. He will not be able to fulfill your request until you stop struggling to save yourself. He will not overrule your will. He will gently wait for you to ask Him for His help. When you surrender all, you will not be disappointed.

FaithStep(s): Pray and surrender all of you and life situations to God. Decide to trust Him for the rest of your life. Write a statement of commitment, trust, and surrrender.

Personal Note: ______________________________

____

____

____

____

____

____

____

____

____

____

____

____

____

____

____

____

Personal Note (cont'd):

Day 34: Rest

Take my yoke upon you, and learn of me; for I am meek and lowly in heart: and ye shall find rest unto your souls. For my yoke is easy, and my burden light. - Matthew 11:29,30

Rest can be received in the physical as well as the spiritual. Physical rest comes from a long and leisurely nap, a soothing bath, or a getaway in the Caribbean Islands. Spiritual rest, on the other hand, can only be received through Christ Jesus. Jesus said, Come unto to me, all ye that labour and are heavy laden, and I will give you rest. Take my yoke upon you, and learn of me; for I am meek and lowly in heart: and ye shall find rest unto your souls (Matthew 11:28,29)." Jesus says in this passage, come to me, take of me, and learn of me.

The rest that Jesus gives can not be compared to any other form of rest. It sets free the mind, body, and soul. The only way to receive this rest is through spending time in prayer, reading of God's word and fellowship with Christ Jesus. This rest is an everlasting rest that maintains a balanced life in the physical as well as the spiritual.

If you want a lasting rest today, you can only receive it when you make up your mind to find the quiet place to enter into the presence of Jesus. During this time you will find out who He is and why He died for you. Rest can be yours just for being in the presence of Jesus Christ; for in His presence is fullness of joy (Psalm 16:11).

FaithStep(s): Take time today to get into the presence of Jesus and receive rest.

Personal Note: ______________________________

Personal Note (cont'd):

Day 35: The Will of God

And be not conformed to this world: but be ye transformed by the renewing of your mind, that ye may prove what is that good, and acceptable, and perfect, will of God. - Romans 12:2

How many times do you say, “I want to know the will of God for my life”? We tend to get frustrated when life is not going the way we think it should. At that point, we begin to wonder if we’re in the will of God. Deuteronomy 29:29 provides a little comfort. It says, “The secret things belong unto the Lord our God: but those things which are revealed belong unto us, and to our children forever, that we may do all the words of this law”. There are secret things that only belong to God and when the time is right, He will reveal them to us. The things He has revealed to us are the things we must submit to doing for His glory.

From this day forward, be not concerned about the secret things that have not been revealed to you. Rather, do those things that you know. When there are things that are of great concern seek God in prayer and through His word. What He makes known are the things you must carry out. His word addresses every circumstance and situation in life. Remember, “We walk by faith not by sight (2 Corinthians 5:7).”

FaithStep(s): Pray each morning for the duty of the day, listen to the guidance of the Holy Spirit, and live in accordance to the well-known commandments already provided.

Personal Note: ______________________________

Personal Note (cont'd): ______________________________

Day 36: I Shall Not Be In Want

Give, and it shall be given unto you; good measure, pressed down, and shaken together, and running over, … - Luke 6:38

The New International Version of the Bible translates Psalm 23:1 as, "The Lord is my shepherd, I shall not be in want." "I shall not be in want" grasped my spirit because all of my life there has been something I wanted that I didn't already possess. What did this really mean? It means when I surrender to Jesus who is my Shepherd, I will trust Him to provide. He will feed me when I hungry, guide me to the path of righteousness, and shield me from all evil. When I surrender to Him, I only want what the will of God is for my life. It is when I step out of God's will that my mind and spirit desire those things that are of the world. It's abiding in the will of God that fulfills every desire.

If your heart is wanting for a physical, emotional, mental or financial desire today, look to Jesus the Shepherd. He will provide your every need. He will direct your path, refresh and restore your life. He will bless you so that you may be a blessing to others. It is when you are a blessing to others that all your needs and wants are met. It's true that if you give, it shall be given to you; good measure, pressed down, and shaken together, and running over

(Luke 6:38). Stay in prayer and confess that "I shall not be in want".

FaithStep(s): Write down all of your wants, find scriptural promises for them, and daily confess that "The Lord is my Shepherd; I shall not be in want of (name the want), I believe it to receive it based upon the Word of God and declare it done in Jesus' name."

Personal Note: ______________________________

____

____

____

____

____

____

____

____

____

____

____

____

____

____

Personal Note (cont'd): ______________________________

Day 37: God Rules by Love

For God so loved the world, that he gave his only begotten Son, that whosoever believeth in him should not perish, but have everlasting life. - John 3:16

God's love is demonstrated in the Bible many times. In fact, God's love, agape, is described in 1 Corinthians 13. "Love suffers long, love rejoices in truth, love bears all things, love believes all things, love hopes all things, love endures all things, and love abides now." God's ultimate love was given when "He gave His only begotten Son that whosoever believes in Him would have everlasting life (John 3:16)." There is nothing God would not do for you because He loves you so much.

How much do you love? How do you love? Compare your love with 1 Corinthians 13 and determine if you have the God kind of love. Agape love casts out all fear (1 John 4:18) and covers a multitude of sins (1 Peter 4:8). There is nothing love can not fix. Walk in love today and receive total freedom.

How can you start walking in love? The moment you recognize a wrong pray for God's love to engulf the person, country, politician, law, or situation. Prayer allows us to live in a large sense and exercise God's love. Prayer has no boundaries and accomplishes more than physical presence. Nothing exists where God is not.

FaithStep(s): Confess God's love for you and others each day. Pray for yourself, your country, nations, world leaders, and the Body of Christ.

Personal Note: ________________________________

____

____

____

____

____

____

____

____

____

____

____

____

____

____

____

____

____

____

Personal Note (cont'd): ______________________________

Day 38: Perfection

It is God that girdeth me with strength, and maketh my way perfect. - Psalm 18:32

Henry Kahlenberg wrote in 1950 "Many of the securities which we thought were solid are crumbling in these critical times." This statement is appropriate today in the 21st Century. The financial structure of America is struggling to stay alive and companies thought to have high standings are folding. Some churches are even under scrutiny. What do we say to all of this? Perfection is found only in God and only the things of God will not change.

In critical times, what can we do? We can remember that God's love will never leave us (Romans 8:38-39), the power of prayer can conquer anything, and Jesus is the same, yesterday, today, and forever (Hebrew 13:8). We can still comfort the poor, feed the hungry, visit the sick, and prisoned (Matthew 25:35-46). Most of all stay true to yourself and your God.

Perfection is found as we develop the Fruit of the Spirit, love, joy, peace, longsuffering, gentleness, goodness, faith, meekness and temperance: against such there is no law (Galatians 5:22-23) in our lives. The world would be a better place for all when people esteem others better than themselves. What step will you take to ensure you are apart of the solution toward a loving world?

FaithStep(s): Each day this week take action to exercise one of the Fruit of the Spirit.

Personal Note: ________________________________

Personal Note (cont'd):

Day 39: The Presence of God

Glory and honour are in his presence; strength and gladness are in his place. - 1 Chronicles 16:27

"God is a Spirit: and they that worship him must worship him in spirit and truth (John 4:24)." We can find God in our worship. As we worship Him in spirit and truth, we become more aware of His presence. Psalm 16:11, "Thou wilt show me the path of life; in thy presence is fullness of joy; at thy right hand there are pleasures for evermore" His presence is the reward for our worship. Many have met God as He healed their sickness, strengthen their weakness, empowered their reality, realized His plan for their life, forgave their sins, and celebrated their victories. His presence is real. He became flesh in Jesus to guide us through all paths of life.

The truth of the matter is God is alive in each one of us. He resides as our Comforter, our Teacher, our Guide, and our Father. The more you surrender to Him through your faith in Jesus Christ; the more you become more like Him. He will walk with you and talk with you along the many paths of life.

If you have the need to experience the presence of God, take the time to get alone, pray to your Father who resides in you by His Spirit, and connect to the power and source of your strength. He is waiting!

FaithStep(s): Spend time today worshipping God and experience His presence as you've never done before.

Personal Note: ______________________________

____

____

____

____

____

____

____

____

____

____

____

____

____

____

____

____

____

____

____

Personal Note (cont'd):

Day 40: Put Away The Idols

And if it seem evil unto you to serve the Lord, choose you this day whom ye will serve; … Joshua 24:15

Many of us refuse to admit we have idols in our lives. Idols? Not me. Webster defines idols as a false god and an object of extreme devotion. How many of us spend more time on a job rather than with our families or with the Body of Christ in worship to Almighty God. Better yet, how much time do you spend doing anything compared to the time you spend in prayer, Bible Study, or helping the less fortunate?

There are many life events in the Old Testament depicting how the Israelites worshipped idols. Even today, there are many religions that worship people, stone statues, stars, moon, etc. None of these can love you, give you peace, or comfort you in time of need. They can not give you eternal life. Eternal life, life forever, is only received when you accept Jesus Christ as the Son of God, His death, burial, and resurrection (Romans 10:9). Decide today whom you will serve and join Joshua as he declared, " but as for me and my house, we will serve the Lord (Joshua 24:15)".

FaithStep(s): Read the entire book of Joshua and Romans.

Personal Note:

Personal Note (cont'd): ________________________________

Afterword

Praise God and to my Lord and Saviour, Jesus Christ! Without the presence of the Father, Son, and Holy Spirit, I would not have completed this work. I am grateful for completion and pray this 40-day experience will bless the lives of all who read these meditations.

There are recurring messages in this book. God, the Father, Son, and Holy Ghost are the thread that keeps them together. Faith, Love, Worship, Obedience, Salvation, Trust and Dependence are a few. Without God being the beginning, center, and end of all our everyday life, we can do nothing. Start each morning with God and end each day with God. That's the only way you will be victorious here on earth. We don't have to be concerned about heaven because Jesus has taken care of heaven for us but we must prepare ourselves in spirit and truth for our transition. How can you receive all that's in heaven if you can't live a holy and righteous life here on earth? No, we won't be perfect until Jesus returns but we can strive to live the best life we can by following the directions of the Holy Spirit by the Holy Word of God.

When I awaken on July 7, 2002 at 3:00AM, I had no idea that this book would be written or completed. When God begin to minister to my heart, the finished work was His desire. His word is true, the steps of a good man is ordered by the Lord

(Psalm 37:23). I don't proclaim I'm good within myself but the goodness and grace of God makes me who I am. You must accept your greatness in God. From the foundation of the earth and the formation of man, He declared all He had done as very good (Genesis 1:31).

It is my sincere hope that this book initiates revolution in your life. I pray that you will renew your spirit and mind about your walk with the Lord, Jesus Christ. Jesus came that you might have life and you might have it more abundantly (John 10:10). Only through an intimate relationship with Him can you achieve abundant life. You are all He says you are, receive it by faith and move into your destiny.

This book is written for all people. It is written for all races, creed, color, and religions. It is also written for those who don't believe in a loving, caring, all-present, all knowing, and all-powerful Divine Being. I guarantee after reading this book you will come to know Him. This book is not about me. It's about that all-present, all-knowing, all-powerful loving Divine Being that wants His ultimate sacrifice to connect you back to Him.

I cannot give praise enough to Jesus Christ for the work He has done and is doing in my life. I pray His continued divine guidance in your life as well. Without others who are on the path to righteousness and reward, the walk is not the same. May your walk in the knowledge and acceptance of one true God build up your most holy faith. May the fruit of the Spirit - love, joy, peace, longsuffering, gentleness, goodness, faith, meekness, and self-control, grows consistently in your walk.

I encourage you to commit to your own 40-day journey into the renewal of your spirit and mind. Your commitment will revolutionize the rest of your life. If you've never had an experience like this, don't put it off. Of course, it is more rewarding when you are lead by the Holy Spirit to do it so I encourage you to pray and seek God's direction for the catalyst for you to grow in your relationship with Him.

40 Days was written out of obedience and to help others to surrender their lives to God. It was written to provide healing and encouragement to those seeking truth. I pray it has accomplished these works in you.

May the God of love, joy, peace, and longsuffering keep you from day to day as He reveals His true character to you. May you walk in your destiny and receive your reward in eternal life. God Bless You!!!!!!!!

40 Days: Scriptural References

Book	Reference
Genesis	5:13
	7:4,12
	7:17
	8:6
	18:28,29
	25:20
	26:34
	32:15
	47:28
	50:3
Exodus	16:35
	24:18
	26:19
	26:21
	34:27
	36:26
Leviticus	25:8
Numbers	1:21
	1:25
	1:41
	2:11
Numbers	2:15
	2:19
	2:28
	13:25
	14:33,34
	26:7
	26:18
	26:41
	32:13
	35:6,7
Deuteronomy	2:7
	8:2,4
	9:9,18
	10:20
	25:3
	29:5
Joshua	4:13
	5:6
	14:7
	14:10
	21:41

40 Days Scriptural References (Cont'd)

Judges	3:11
	5:8
	5:31
	8:28
	12:14
	13:1
1 Samuel	4:18
	17:16
2 Samuel	2:10
	5:4
	10:18
	15:7
1 Kings	2:11
	4:26
	6:17
	7:3
	7:38
	11:42
	14:21
	15:10
	19:8
2 Kings	2:24
2 Kings	8:9
	10:14
	12:1
	14:23
1 Chronicles	5:18
	12:36
	19:18
	29:27
2 Chronicles	9:30
	12:13
	22:2
	24:1
Ezra	2:8
	2:10
	2:24,25
	2:34
	2:38
	2:64
	2:66
Nehemiah	5:15
	7:13
	7:15

40 Days Scriptural References (Cont'd)

Nehemiah	7:28,29	Acts	1:3
	7:36		4:22
	7:41		7:23
	7:44		7:30
	7:62		7:36
	7:66-68		7:42
	9:21		13:18
	11:13		13:21
Job	42:16		23:13
Psalm	95:10		23:21
Jeremiah	52:30	2 Corinthians	11:24
Ezekiel	4:6	Hebrews	3:9
	29:11-13		3:17
	41:2	Revelations	7:14
	46:22		11:2
Amos	2:10		13:5
	5:25		14:1
Jonah	3:4		14:3
Matthew	4:2		21:17
Mark	1:13		
Luke	4:2		
John	3:4		

Subject Index

This following Subject Index is a guide for those who would like to locate a special topic of interest. The number next to the subject is the designation for the page the topic appears.

W

Suggested Reading:

Call To Conquer - Bishop Eddie L. Long

Women Devotional Bible - New International Version

God's Calling - A. J. Russell

Acts of Faith - Iyanla Vanzant

Tapping The Power Within - Iyanla Vanzant

Sister to Sister - Volume 1 and 2 - Rev. Dr. Suzan Johnson Cook
Edited by Linda H. Hollies

Sister Strength - Rev. Dr. Suzan Johnson Cook

God's Little Daily Devotional - Honor Books

Light For My Path - HumbleCreek, Inspiration For Life

Sister Wit - Jacqueline Jakes

My Utmost For His Highest - Oswald Chambers

Young's Analytical Concordance - Robert Young, LL.D.

My Soul's Surrender - Phenessa A. Gray

Experiencing God - Henry Y. Blackaby and Claude King

"Phenessa A. Gray, From The Foreword"

The main themes of this devotional journal are (1) ***God's word*** is the answer to all your problems and concerns, (2) ***God's presence*** is more important than anything, and (3) ***God's provisions*** are manifested through seed, time, and harvest. I pray that you will find each reading a point of inspiration for all your needs! If you are looking for a way to spend more time with the Lord, this journal will help you. This 40-Day journey is being shared with all that need encouragement to listen to the Spirit within you and to dedicate time to receive direction for your life. On each page, you are given a "Faith Step" and space to write down your commitments or thoughts. "***Carlond Gray, From the Forward***"

About The Author

Carlond W. Gray is a native of Pensacola, FL and the mother of Phenessa A. Gray, author of My Soul's Surrender and What's This Prospect Research?. She received her education at Nova University where she earned her Master of Business Administration degree and a Master of Project Management degree from Keller Graduate School. She completed a two-year program in Biblical Studies at The City of Hope Bible Institute in conjunction with the International Bible Institute in Sante Fe Springs, CA.

Carlond W. Gray now resides in Atlanta, GA where she is a member of New Birth Missionary Baptist Church where Bishop Eddie L. Long is Senior Pastor. She has a heart after God and a passion for biblical teaching and service to others.

www.ingramcontent.com/pod-product-compliance
Ingram Content Group UK Ltd.
Pitfield, Milton Keynes, MK11 3LW, UK
UKHW040015200726
13854UKWH00001B/215

9 781418 421243